SCHOOLING YOUR BOSS TO NOT SUCK™

BY ERIC MUSS-BARNES

BY ERIC MUSS-BARNES

Cover designed and created by Eric Muss-Barnes

Bound and Printed by www.CreateSpace.com

For More Information Please Visit:
www.SchoolingYourBossToNotSuck.com

International Standard Book Number (ISBN): 978-1460980033

PRINTED AND MANUFACTURED IN

THE UNITED STATES OF AMERICA

First International Printing: March 2011

this book is respectfully dedicated to
WALTER ELIAS DISNEY

Although Walt Disney passed away before I was even born, I admire him enough to sincerely believe, he would have been the greatest boss ever. If I could have worked for him, I would have never endured the bosses who compelled me to write this book in the first place!

MY HEARTFELT SPECIAL THANKS
TO THE FOLLOWING PEOPLE WHO DO NOT SUCK

Lynne Volk, for inadvertently providing me the inspiration to write this book. After giving me a copy of a very "short but sweet" business book which has sold millions of copies, I realized I had ideas that could fit a similar format. If it hadn't been for reading that, this book you're holding would not exist. I'm not banking on this book selling dozens, let alone millions, however, Lynne, if it sells millions, I'll buy you a car... but who am I kidding? Realistically, I'll be lucky if it earns enough cash to buy you a hamburger.

Ray Harris, for being awesomesauce. I long resented Ray, because he was the first person to ever lay me off from a job. Simultaneously, I also have the warmest respect and admiration for Ray, because he was the first person to ever make me feel I was truly invaluable and essential to a company. Many of the positive lessons I learned in this book came from working with him. I haven't seen Ray in over a decade, yet he remains the coolest person I ever worked with (except my 3rd grade bestfriend, whom I helped get about 3 or 4 jobs for over the years).

Rick Santich, for hiring me into my first job after I completed my first novel. Possessing only a highschool education, it was a nightmare trying to find employment after I wrote my book. I couldn't find a good job, because I lacked a college degree. I couldn't find a crappy job, because once employers discovered I was a novelist, they said, "You wrote a novel? Oh, you'll only be here 3 months and find something better. No point in hiring you." I was seen as too uneducated for quality employment and too ambitious for menial work. After 9 months of filling out applications everyday, Rick believed in me and gave me my big break.

Danny Blitz, for being a true rockstar of a boss. Danny not only hired me at a moment when I was desperate for work, but he proved to be a noble and loyal friend as the years went by. He always called me a "God Among Men" for my work and I recall the day I resigned my position, he looked genuinely depressed. That was very touching. No one had ever reacted so emotionally when I left any other job. I may be a God Among Men, but he really is a rockstar. Literally. How many people can say their boss had a video on MTV? Danny Blitz rocks in more ways than one.

Bob Weil, Sam Smith, Paul Meyers, and Emily Brewer, for their collective responsibility in hiring me into the best job of my life, at the humble little company I aspire to retire from.

Finally, thanks to *The Cleveland Press* newspaper, for teaching me at the age of 11 that "job security" is an illusion and does not exist anywhere. Not even in a company that is over a century old.

 INTRODUCTION

Dear Boss Of Whomever Gives You This Book,

Please don't fire your employee for giving you this book. Your employee doesn't think you suck. Your employee just wants to prevent you from starting to suck.

Respectfully,

Eric Muss-Barnes

P.S. Okay, maybe your employee does think you suck, but let's just keep that between the two of us. Don't let them know I told you.

PROLOGUE

"My boss sucks!"

How many times have we heard that phrase? Whether from friends, family, fellow workers, or our own mouths, we have all heard those words spoken on countless occasions.

Wouldn't it be great to have a boss who didn't suck? How cool would it be to have a boss who was more superhero than supervillain? What if you had a boss who took the time to listen to the needs and desires of his/her employees, instead of attending some outlandishly expensive seminar where other-bosses-who-suck give bad advice to your already-sucky-boss making them an even-more-sucky-boss whilst under the guise of "leveraging more effective leadership" or somesuch malarkey? Blech! What a crock!

Such notions were the inspiration for this book.

Although, I have to be honest, before I set out to spin this yarn, the biggest "internal conflict" I faced was the thought, "Why bother?"

With thousands of books in the world on managerial skills, who would care about mine? Would anyone even notice my book exists in the sea of others?

Then I realized something important. Something distinctive that would set mine apart from all the rest.

Namely?

It's quite simple...

I'm not a boss.

I don't manage anyone. I don't have a college degree. I'm nothing more than a proverbial grunt. A metaphorical foot soldier. One of the pawns. A "low man on the totem pole" as they say. In other words, I'm a lot like you. That was the moment it hit me - being an "Everyman" is exactly *why* my advice matters! Therein lies the distinction and the strength of this book. I'm not a Ph.D. with decades of managerial experience in Fortune 100 companies. I'm not making 6 figures and cruising around in a car that costs more than your house. I'm meat and potatoes, like all you good people.

I thought, "Maybe I could write a fun and inspirational book about managing people, one that appeals to common folks, and we can share it with our bosses!"

Lacking fancy accolades and ivy league education, what makes me qualified to comment on business strategy and managing people? Absolutely nothing. Other than the fact that I have decades of experience in "water cooler conversations" around the workplace - I pay attention. I listen. I know precisely what sort of a boss people loathe and I know exactly what kind of a boss earns respect.

Some bosses think they don't need to be respected, as long as employees do what they are told. Those bosses suck. They are also ignorant and ineffective, because anyone with half a brain can tell you, people work much harder when working for leadership they respect, as opposed to a chump they resent.

I've worked with lots of respectable ladies and gentlemen.

I've also worked with lots of chumps.

That is what makes me qualified. As they say, "When you have a good story on your hands, you are obligated to speak for people who have no voice."

In the world of managerial seminars and advice books, employees never have a voice. Employees never have an opportunity to school their bosses on how to not suck. So I decided to create that opportunity and speak for those who never have a chance.

Bosses don't need to school each other on how to be effective leaders.

No.

We common folk are the ones who must educate our bosses on how to motivate us.

That is where the authors of competing "managerial advice" books all fail! Authors of those books are leaders and educators with masters degrees and years of experience as bosses. You find it insulting that your boss attends those expensive seminars? Heck, the authors of those other books are the ones who teach those exorbitant seminars! Seminars which cost your company more money than your yearly salary at the last job you were laid off from! What do those leaders know about their followers? Kings educating fellow kings is nothing more than the blind leading the blind! Few things are more annoying to the masses than watching oppressive leaders patting themselves on the back and congratulating each other on what a great job they are doing.

Those bosses suck too. Bigtime.

"What a ruler truly needs," I thought, "is to be commanded by their subjects, dictating what we require from our leadership."

I know. Your boss is a jackass on a powertrip, so he/she won't respond to that attitude. Don't worry. I'll make him/her think they are in charge. I'll say something like, "What a ruler truly needs is to have their humble subjects make desperate pleas for mercy." Something like that. Your powertripping boss will dig that. We'll trick them into reading this if we have to.

Why the snarky attitude? Because that's the way people truly behave. That is how we talk around the watercooler. The "sunshine and rainbows and puppydogs" attitude of other advice books is not realistic. As it was said in the film *Chaplin,* many working-class folks are poor and they enjoy seeing the well-to-do getting razzed a bit. People have enjoyed that for centuries and they will for centuries to come. If that helps improve things, why not? I'm paraphrasing, of course, but that was the gist of it.

Hence, the idea for "Schooling Your Boss to not Suck" was born.

I won't lie to you. This book isn't going to be a source of profound revelations. You won't read this and encounter a philosophy you've never heard of before. The concepts I discuss are most likely things you've heard about in the past. However, I aspired to eliminate all the extraneous ideas and distill the vital information down into simply consolidated topics. I speak from real life experience in telling you what works - and what doesn't work - in regard to getting people to deliver their personal best in the workplace.

At the end of each chapter, I divide the concept into one of two categories - retention or efficiency.

Why?

Because assuming a company offers products and services that are desirable by the public and marketed properly, the best way to maintain a solid internal framework at a company boils down to those two simple ideas; Retaining exceptional personnel and their doing efficient work. Overly simplified, perhaps. Nevertheless, for those bosses who focus on the bottom line, you'll be able to see at a glance why the advice in each chapter is relevant.

Concepts in each chapter are reflected in positive stories about great bosses, who did things the right way, and negative stories, about bosses who sucked. Sometimes they sucked eggs. Sometimes they sucked the poo-stained rectal hair from the corpse of a month-dead Bigfoot.

"Baby? Um... This book isn't going to get you fired, will it?" That was the first question my girlfriend asked when I told her about it.

"You've worked too hard to get where you are." She said. "Isn't it kind of risky to write a book like this?"

"What? Oh, no, no, no." I reassured her. "It's not like that at all. The people I work with and my current boss are all really cool. In fact, I never mention my current job or any current coworkers anywhere in the book. Believe me, there is no need to! I have plenty of stories from former bosses to fill a book! Plus, not only do I never talk about my current employer, but in the stories I *do* tell, I never reveal any real names of people or companies either. I use pseudonyms for everything."

My stories may be real experiences, but I am diplomatic enough to maintain some decorum regarding the details!

Truth be known, I've reached a point in my life where I work with great people in an incredibly rewarding environment that affords me the chance to achieve countless aspirations. The people I work with all "get it" and already practice the suggestions I make in this text. Everyday, I thank goodness that I have been blessed with a true "dream job" and the world-class bosses and coworkers to go along with it. But, believe me, I endured a lot of sucky bosses to get where I am today.

Although I strive to be entertaining, and this book maintains a very lighthearted and sarcastic tone, the underlying messages are serious ones. Being an effective leader doesn't need to be complicated. While I jokingly maintain an "us versus them" attitude throughout the text (those "sucky-bosses" against the "righteous-employees") the truth is - we all have bosses! Therefore, we're all in this together, folks. Even if you have no official "subordinates" we all have different levels of experience and seniority. We all have ladies and gentlemen "above" and "below" us on the totem pole. No matter where you stand on that totem pole, I hope this book will offer you some beneficial food for thought and allow you to garner knowledge of simple principals that will make your workplace more fulfilling and, by extension, make your life more rewarding.

After all, you're stuck dealing with those goofballs for 8 hours a day! While you may never become best pals with your boss, hopefully you can at least reach a point where you don't dread being around them!

School your boss to be a decent human being (you wouldn't have picked up a book with that title though). Maybe you'll manage to school yourself a little in the process too. No matter what your background, no matter where you come from, I'm sure we can all agree - life is far more enjoyable when people aren't sucking.

CHAPTER ONE

"Hire people smarter than you and let them do their job."
- Anonymous

Longevity in retaining quality employees stems from appreciating the skills people have. Others will often have more knowledge than you. Don't feel intimidated by that. As a boss, your job is to empower your team to accomplish their work. Let them honestly work to deliver a job. You are not there under the expectation of being smarter than everyone else. Therefore, don't feel threatened by having people with more talent or intellect than your own. Your role is that of a facilitator, not a dictator.

I lied.

Remember in the prologue when I said I wasn't a boss or a manager? That's not true. There was one very brief period in my life - for a mere year or two - when I was the Creative Director for an Internet video company. We were a small operation (that sounded vaguely like Lando Calrissian - so let's pretend the company was called Cloud City) and there were very few employees, but, I was a boss over 2 people and I was in charge of hiring them.

When we started Cloud City, I was a "Jack of All Trades" and did everything from shooting and editing our video production work, to graphic design for our magazine advertisements, to programming our website. As we gained more funding and the time came to hire more personnel to alleviate some of my workload, the owner of the company permitted me to hire ladies and gentlemen into whatever roles I wanted. Whatever I enjoyed doing the most, I would get to continue doing. The responsibilities I enjoyed the least, I could delegate out and manage people in those positions.

Honestly, I loved it all. The diversity was a blast. There really wasn't an element among my job responsibilities which I disliked. I even used the studio space on the weekends for my own photography and art projects. Sweet deal. Fantastic experience. I will say, the thing I loved doing the most was the video production. My weakpoint was programming.

Back in gradeschool, my bestfriend Morpheus (he's a white dude, but I couldn't resist calling him that during his 30s, after he shaved his head like Laurence Fishburne in *The Matrix*) and I were the first "computer geeks" in our class. We'd stay after school for hours, learning all we could in the computer lab. In highschool, we took a beginning computer class that was so simplistic for us, we basically invented our own curriculum so we wouldn't be bored out of our minds. Ever tried to write a program that prints any input in Pig Latin? Atthay asway uroay irstfay rojectpay.

High school computer geek humor.

More than a decade later, I had become a pretty respectable graphic designer and he had become quite a talented programmer.

Around that time, I was working a graphic design job at a company that was nearly an hour from home. When job hunting for a position that would provide a shorter commute, I came across a design/programming position that would only be 15 minutes away at Generic Computer Company. Perfect! (No, they weren't really called that, but if I don't start giving these places names, you're gonna get confused.)

So anyway, I landed the interview, but after meeting with Generic Computer Company, I knew darned well I wasn't qualified for the job. The person who was interviewing me knew it too. As I was leaving, I mentioned Morpheus to them.

"My friend is unemployed and looking for work right now. He's a much more skilled programmer than I am. Maybe he'd be a better fit for the position. I could have him call you." I offered.

Morpheus called and got the job.

Three months later, the graphic designer at Generic Computer Company quit and Morpheus suggested they hire me. They did. As a result, Morpheus and I worked together for a good 2 years at that place.

During that tenure, I learned an immense amount about programming. In fact, by the time I left that position, I knew far more than Morpheus knew when he started. Of course, since Morpheus was programming all day and I was only dabbling, he remained twice as competent as me.

Okay. Back to the Cloud City job.

As much as I enjoyed programming in my Creative Director position, I knew Morpheus was better than I was.

He was the first person I decided to hire.

When I finally convinced Morpheus to leave his job at Generic Computer Company and come work for me, I gave him all the freedom he needed. In fact, he didn't write a single line of code for over a week. I told him I wanted him to construct the system in the most efficient way possible. Therefore, I wanted him to take all the time he required and plan it out properly. He spent day after day writing, sketching, refining, asking me questions. I recall Morpheus apologizing to me and acting all nervous - as if I'd be mad at him for not building any webpages yet.

The architecture of websites is like the architecture of a building. You have to plan it properly and have solid blueprints before you begin construction. If you have shoddy blueprints and you make too many changes to your design after construction has begun, the project will become far more costly and time-consuming than if you planned it properly in the first place. If you build your whole house and suddenly discover you forgot to install a bathroom, it's going to be incredibly expensive to retrofit one into a finished home, compared to constructing it during the original build. Right?

I kept on explaining to Morpheus, "I want this to be the best work you can make. Take your time. We have a working website and we can leave it up and running as long as we need to. I want what you build to be the best thing you've created. So, plan it out properly and don't start building it until you're ready."

That is the way every boss should be. I trusted him. I practiced what I preach - I hired someone smarter than me and I let him do his job. I didn't bother him. I didn't criticize him. I didn't judge him. I didn't rush him or pester him. I had faith that he was planning and researching and constructing something with far greater skill than I could.

Sure enough, in the end, he built a fantastic application with features beyond what I was capable of creating.

(On a side note, I recall telling that story to an awful boss of mine in California many years later. He laughed at me and said he would never allow a programmer to sit around and not write code for a week. I just shook my head. Needless to say, the braindead loser knew nothing about programming and could barely send an email without assistance.)

Sorry. Was that harsh? I warned you that I'm a snarky Average Joe. I'm not going to be the stuffy "politically correct" author and say nice things about sleazebags. I won't go into details of *why* he was sleazy. Just take my word for it before I digress too much.

Where was I? Ah, yes. Cloud City.

As I said, my favorite aspect of my Creative Director position was the video work, so the next person I hired at Cloud City was a graphic designer.

That became my first experience with doing job interviews.

Wow. That could make a whole other book!

I know this book is about schooling bosses, but, let me just interject - to any potential employees out there, don't be a gloomy cynic in your job interviews! I was shocked how many people walked in the door being negative and depressed. It was really shocking and weird. Very glum lot. Then again, it was Cleveland. Maybe it was the weather.

But I digress again.

The graphic designer I hired was a very talented young woman. Again, far more talented than me. That was the whole point. I did my best to stay out of her way and let her do her job. As it should be.

Unlike most of the pansy middle managers of the corporate world, who feel threatened by subordinates of superior intellect, I reveled in knowing my employees were smarter than me. As a result, we all looked great to the owner of the company. The employees did a great job. I proved that I hired the right people. Everyone wins.

You're not paying attention are you?

Oh. I get it.

You still want to know why I called that one guy a sleazebag, don't you?

Man, come on!

That has nothing to do with this story. This is my first business book. If I go off on some unrelated tangent in the first chapter of my first business book, no one will take me seriously! I have to stick to the topic! (I know, I design a business book that has a comic book cover and *now* I demand to be taken seriously?)

(sigh)

Okay. I'll tell you. I don't blame you. I'm the same way. Someone just "hints" at the story and you want to hear the whole thing.

Okay. Fine. Here is why the guy was sleazy.

There is not much to the story, honestly. He gave me a ton of freedom. He wasn't the sort who needed to "let me do my job" or tried to micro-manage things. Not at all. He was great in that regard. Never did he stand in my way. The whole time, he was incredibly supportive and helpful and provided me with all the resources I required to do my work. I was very grateful to him for all of that. He was awesome in terms of letting me do my job.

However, the guy totally lied to me.

He hired me as a "full-time employee" but the moment I finished building his new company website, I was let go. I had even confronted him on that point during the original job interview. My gut instinct told me not to trust him.

"Are you sure you need me full time? This sounds more like temporary contract work." I said.

"No, no." He assured me. "I need you to build the site, but there is still a ton of other work to do after that."

Riiiiight. I smelled a rat. But, hey, I needed the money, so I went along with it. He told me I was a part of the company, I'd still have lots of opportunities once the website was finished, and I'd have hula girls and a Jacuzzi in my office.

Okay, he didn't actually promise hula girls or a Jacuzzi.

He did show me the door the day after I finished his website though. Just like I knew he would. Lucky for me, I had sent out job applications the day before, landed an interview the following day, and therefore I was only unemployed for about 48 hours.

Pays to trust your instincts.

Now let me get back to the subject of this chapter! You're making me go off on useless tangents! That story had nothing to do with schooling your boss. That guy could really only fit into a chapter called "Don't be a Lying Scumwad" and I kind of assume that isn't a chapter which is required. Hopefully, it's self-evident to never outright lie to people.

Definitely a supervillain, that guy.

Back to the topic at hand, I had a boss who did not follow the philosophy of hiring people smarter than him and letting them do their job. He hired people smarter than him and made them do trivial jobs. We'll call him Mr. Phonysmile.

Mr. Phonysmile was one of those bosses who always plastered on one of those fake sympathetic grins while he was condescending to you like a child in preschool.

Oh? You've worked for him too, huh?

Yeah, we all worked for that rotten Mr. Phonysmile at one time or another.

He was the type of person who would never let me get ahead in my job. We worked in a digital printing company, so there were countless opportunities for advancing into different roles and learning new skills and new equipment. I learned a lot, but not as much as I should have been learning, if Mr. Phonysmile had been giving me better opportunities.

Now, honestly, I didn't even notice at the time. I didn't really care. I came to work. I did my job. I wasn't looking for more responsibility. I just did my thing. I'm rather young and naive in a lot of ways, but I was even more young and naive back then. I was totally ignorant of how much I was being underutilized at that company, until the assistant manager of our department pointed it out to me one day.

"I don't see why Mr. Phonysmile hired that new guy. I told Mr. Phonysmile he should put you in that position. You're way more competent than the new guy anyway!" The assistant manager told me.

"Oh?" I said, totally oblivious.

"Yes!" The assistant manager said. "And he's paying him almost twice what you're making!"

WHAT!? Okay. That got my attention. Now I was kind of miffed too!

While the assistant manger recognized my value, Mr. Phonysmile never afforded me the chance to really show what I was capable of doing. I was just micro-managed into doing menial tasks. Now, I'm happy to do menial tasks. Someone has to do them. I'm not so arrogant to say those jobs were beneath me. Nonetheless, I was capable of a whole lot more.

When I left that job, the assistant manager took me aside and told me how proud he was of me. He said, "I'm shocked that you stayed here this long. You're better than this place anyway. Mr. Phonysmile doesn't appreciate that. But I can see it. You're going to go far, Eric."

Again, my humility didn't permit me to believe that at the time. I thought he was just being kind.

In retrospect, considering what I have accomplished, compared to where I was back then, he was right about me after all. I have done quite a bit more with my life than printing out banners for garbage trucks. Once I found opportunities to be hired in places that appreciated my capabilities and let me do my job, I was able to thrive.

As a boss, you will have people like that.

They know more than you. Be okay with that. Trust their advice. Trust their input. Allow them the freedom to determine their own workflows and procedures and practices. Have faith in their competence until they prove otherwise.

Even when I hired people, I tried to follow that philosophy. I was a facilitator. I was there to help. I was there to assist and give advice and guidance. Never did I tell anyone how things had to be done. Never did I attempt to impose my own methodologies on others. I simply offered my opinions and trusted my employees to make the best decisions. After all, that is why they were there.

Everyone knows the governing precept in geometry which states - "The shortest distance between any two points is a straight line."

Right?

Any smart person can tell you that.

No.

The shortest distance between any two points... is to ignore the distance.

Allow for that. Allow for people who are able to see things differently. People who bring a unique perspective. People with a different kind of "smarts" to add to your team.

Find people who think different. Act different. Work different. Then trust them to do their jobs.

NOT SUCKING SUGGESTION #1:

Trust that the people you work with know more than you. Instead of being threatened by that, celebrate the fact! They should know more than you. That means you hired the right people. Help them. Have faith in them. Give them what they need. Hire people smarter than you and let them do their job.

THE BOTTOM LINE

(How does this advice translate into profits?)

Respect the competence and skills and experience of people. Don't assume you are smarter than them. Assume they are smarter than you. Thereby improving retention of quality people, which translates into increased profits.

CHAPTER TWO

"The Romans didn't build an Empire by sitting around having meetings, they did it by killing everyone who opposed them."

- Anonymous

Do some actual work as a boss beyond making charts and having meetings. That is not doing work. In fact, endless meetings and meaningless charts and graphs are the most ideal way to avoid doing any genuine work. Plan. Gather your data. Study the information. Those tasks are of critical importance. But don't worry about storyboarding every single frame of your movie! You need to start shooting.

While working at a small startup Internet Video Company in Ohio, the owner of the business (we'll call him Mr. Cooldude) was asked to preside over another company. Interested in the new position, but not wishing to shut down his own business, Mr. Cooldude decided to hire a new president for his Internet Video Company.

Mr. Cooldude, as the name suggests, was a cool guy.

The new president?

Not so much.

As the second employee at the Internet Video Company, (no, that wasn't the real name either - try to stay with me) I knew the business inside and out. We had fantastic technology involving streaming video content over the web for business clients, a full decade before YouTube ever existed. We were offering stellar services and cutting-edge innovations, far ahead of our time. We just happened to be very weak in the sales and marketing department. Like so many technology geeks, we knew how to build something awesome... we just had no clue how to sell it. Especially during an age when no one had broadband!

That was where the new president guy came in. Let's call him Mr. Assfog (not his real name either, believe it or not). Now, supposedly, good old Mr. Assfog was some kind of marketing expert and salesman who had a backlog of potential clients and could sell, sell, SELL our way to an early and wealthy retirement! (Obviously, it didn't pan out that way, or I'd be sitting on a beach in the tropics with a supermodel right now, instead of sitting at a computer, writing this book for you nice folks.)

Mr. Assfog was one of those "graphs and charts" people. Ah, yes, the scourge of charts, graphs and acronyms. He liked to draw diagrams and little pyramids and things. Reminiscent of a kindergartner. Cute when you're 5 years old. Not as endearing when you're over 30 and running a business.

My fellow employees and I learned this fact one afternoon when Mr. Assfog called us into his office at the end of his first week.

"Hey, do you guys have a minute?" he asked. "I want to show you something I've been working on."

The rest of my team was very excited! Mr. Assfog sounded so enthused! Surely he was going to outline a sales strategy for us. Right? That is why he was hired, after all. Possibly, he'd have some text and guidelines for creating some sales materials for the graphics person. Surely, he'll show us a draft of some scripts he prepared for promotional videos, so the video producer could shoot a commercial or two. Maybe, there would be a few email leads from former clients he had contacted at other companies. Would he maybe have a contract or two already lined up? Perhaps a demo scheduled for a major corporation?

We were very excited!

Did he have any of those things?

No.

None of that.

You know what the guy had to show us?

A pyramid chart.

Seriously.

He sat in his office 8 hours a day for an entire week and had produced nothing but a freaking useless pyramid chart!?

Not just any pyramid chart, mind you - a pyramid chart outlining his ideas for our organizational structure.

THERE WERE THREE EMPLOYEES! WE DIDN'T NEED AN ORGANIZATIONAL STRUCTURE!

"See?" he announced proudly. "I came up with this foundation for our webcasts. We have our overall business at the bottom. Then above that are the structures for programming and all the production work. So, as we hire more teams, they will fall into these categories. Then we have the managerial teams we'll be able to bring into place above that level. And since you three are here the longest, you'll be able to roll up into these positions. Along the top there's the final sales teams and they'll be capped by our client and executive structure."

Okay?

We were all baffled.

What on earth was this man smoking?

Organizational structure. Seriously? For a company with THREE employees!? Was this moron on drugs!? We didn't need this fool to provide us with an outline of job responsibilities. THERE WERE THREE OF US! We knew what our jobs were! Programming. Design and video production. Sales. That was all. That was what the three of us did. The question was - what was this joker-of-a-president doing!? NOTHING! He was drawing pictures in his office!

"Okay," I said. "And how does this help us to get sales? Where do we get clients by having this little chart?"

He didn't like me much after I called him out like that.

Was he talking with us employees? Was he making an effort to learn our business? Was he attempting to understand our technology? Was he meeting with our salesperson to understand what leads he had? Was he meeting with me to understand how our broadcasting system functioned? Was he meeting with our programmer to understand how the client login on the website functioned? No. The idiot was trying to structure a company that he knew nothing about and required no restructuring! He was talking expansion and teams for what purpose!? We were making no money! Why on earth would you expand the production personnel when we had no client base that required additional people in the first place!?

We got news for you buddy - we don't start making a profit and we won't have the cash to hire the personnel you are organizing into your stupid little pyramid. Screw your charts! First things first. What we needed was to drum up business. To get sales! To have clients. If he couldn't help with that, he was useless. Unless of course we started offering babysitting for kindergartners to make ends meet - then maybe we'd let this nimrod pull out his crayons and color little pyramids with the kids.

Want to be a boss who doesn't suck? Lose the charts. Lose the diagrams. Drop the acronyms and the doubletalk. We don't care. We know you are full of it.

That was the most important lesson I learned from that experience - bosses who make too many charts are not to be trusted.

Seriously.

They don't actually do any real work. They just shuffle things around and make new charts and lay out new graphs and create the illusion of fostering change - when in fact, they don't know the first thing about real work. They just pull proverbial wool over the eyes and blow fog up your sphincter. Beware the Mr. Assfogs of the world.

Saddest part is, I know he meant well. He wasn't *trying* to be a useless hunk of dead weight. He was simply brainwashed by those inane corporate dogmas into honestly believing he was doing real work.

Don't get me wrong. I understand the value in planning and plotting your course. That is essential in everything from running a business, to reading the blueprints for building a house, to pulling out the instruction manual when you hook up your new home entertainment center. Charts and diagrams and plans are viable and important tools for countless situations.

In fact, Walt Disney (have I established how much I admire him?), invented the notion of creating a storyboard for structuring movies. Brilliant. I've used storyboards on my films and outlines on my novels. Believe me, I appreciate the value of laying out the strategy and organizing the data at hand. I've never successfully finished writing a book without establishing that sort of blueprint ahead of time.

But there is a huge difference between storyboarding a film versus spending a week constructing a pyramid chart for a company with 3 employees. The former is necessary, so the film crew can understand the days work. The latter is only done by preschool children who just learned how to hold a crayon.

Meetings are crucial.

Charts and graphs are a fantastic way to disseminate information quickly and efficiently.

You should still have meetings.

Still create charts.

But remember this - charts and meetings are like donuts. Delicious if they are quality treats you quickly scarf down on rare occasions. Disgusting if they are cheap junk, and you are strapped into a chair like Alex in *A Clockwork Orange*, and they are jammed down your throat for an hour.

Make your charts and meetings the good donuts.

Not the horror movie donuts.

(I realize *A Clockwork Orange* is not a horror film. More of a dystopian character study. I'm simply making an analogy. Work with me here.)

NOT SUCKING SUGGESTION #2:

Stop with all the charts and the meetings. Constantly attempting to meet and diagram and organize and plan and refine just makes things more disorganized. You have intelligent people working for you. Show them the plan and permit them to move on. Remember, the Romans. They built an Empire by actions, not meetings... and they likely lost the Empire by having too many meetings and not enough action! Take that chart and shove it, it ain't workin' here no more!

THE BOTTOM LINE

(How does this advice translate into profits?)

The old saying among carpenters is, "Measure twice, cut once." The saying isn't, "Measure 50 times, cut once." Spending more time "doing" and less time "planning" will produce faster results. Thereby improving efficiency, which translates into increased profits.

CHAPTER THREE

"You don't 'act' noble. You don't 'act' chivalric. You *are* noble. You *are* chivalrous. Or you're not. But it's never an act. It's who you are... Or it isn't."

- Anonymous

Empowering employees is a cliche and it stems from treating people as noble and ethical and competent. The more you choose to take power and authority away from employees, the more you prove you have no faith in your people. Trust them. Give them the resources to truly excel at their job.

Surely everyone can relate to this - you walk into a store to purchase something and some poor minimum-wage cashier is forced to call over a manager to "clear the register" because some sort of error was made when ringing up an order.

Why?

These mistakes happen all the time. Why does the manager need to be called every single time the cashier makes a mistake?

Why can't the cashier be trusted and empowered to do their job? Why can't the cashier clear the error themselves? Why inconvenience the customers who just want to buy their merchandise and get the heck out of there?! Why does a "higher authority" have to intervene?

If you ask the company owners, we know the lies they would give. They would talk about things like "efficiency" and "assisting" and "liability" and other terms that skirt the real issue. We all know the true answer - They think their cashiers are thieves.

As customers and employees we all see these "policies" for what they really are. Namely, there are only one of two possibilities for why the cashier isn't empowered to clear the register transaction themselves:

1. The company is employing cashiers who are criminals and idiots.

2. The company is employing cashiers who are decent and intelligent... but treating them like criminals and idiots.

This is similar to stores which require all customers to check their packages at the door. Excuse me? I don't own a car - only a motorcycle. Hence, when I shop in a store, I have to bring a backpack. I'm expected to hand over my innocuous personal property to enter your store? Why?

We know the answer - because those companies have a corporate policy to presume all their customers are thieves.

The moment I saunter into a store and some $7/hour rent-a-cop asks for my backpack, I smile and say, "I don't give business to stores that assume their customers are criminals." Then I turn around, walk out, and spend my money elsewhere.

Or I just ignore them and keep walking into the store, pretending they don't exist. That's fun because it really gets on their nerves!

But I digress.

Let's get back to the powerless cashier.

"Empowerment" is a word you see tossed around a lot within the managerial advice tomes. Evidently, it gets repeated so frequently because so few bosses still understand what it means.

When you get right down to it, empowerment is a question of trust. Does the boss trust their employee to handle the requirements of the job? Or not?

By extension, any matter of "employee trust" is also a question of a bosses competence. Did the boss hire trustworthy people? Or not?

"Empowerment" simply means giving the employee the authority to accomplish things in the workplace without requiring "permissions" and "approvals" from a dozen different bosses, just so the employee can change a roll of toilet paper! Or clear a cash register transaction.

Often times, a boss will complain when employees fail to take responsibility for their actions. Heck, that is a common complaint among all of our culture! People frequently fail to take responsibility for their actions. We see it all the time. You know the type. Everything that goes wrong in their life is the fault of somebody else. Some dimwit buys hot coffee, spills the hot coffee on her lap, then sues the restaurant for getting burned with hot coffee.

Pathetic.

The first step to making people take responsibility for their actions is to make them feel totally empowered. Show them they are in control. Lack of empowerment too easily provides the excuse to take no responsibility.

"It's not my fault, because I wasn't allowed to..."

"It's not my fault, because they didn't let me..."

If you want people to take responsibility for their actions, make sure they feel empowered.

When a blue collar worker needs a new tool, he should just be able to buy one. No approvals. No permissions. Just get him the tool. If the boss, Mr. Idiotface, expects the employee to "justify" the expense, maybe the boss should get out of his Ivory Tower and understand the needs of the workers.

I once worked for a real jerkhole who wouldn't let me do my job either.

Somewhere in a backwoods small town of northern Ohio, I found myself working at an enormous tradeshow company. We actually designed, built, and even archived mammoth tradeshow displays for major corporations. So, when a company spends $2 million on a tradeshow booth with multiple floors, and massive displays, and posters, and tons of glass and steel, we made that stuff. A fascinating business, we had a gargantuan warehouse storing all the tradeshow booths of past clients, a huge construction area full of blue collar union workers, and a front office of white collar salesmen and draftsmen and designers. This crazy hustle and bustle was all located under a single roof of one gigantic warehouse.

I had a particular love for the behemoth storage area. That football field of wooden crates always made me think of the end of *Raiders of the Lost Ark*. Literally. It really looked like that. Wooden crates two stories high stretching into the distance with dim pools of light between the skinny alleyways. I was convinced the Ark of the Covenant was stashed away in there someplace. We'll call the company "Top Men" in honor of Indiana Jones.

Some of the more commonly recycled posters and banners at Top Men were kept in a smaller storage area, right outside the doors of the graphic design department.

I was tasked with an overwhelming project which had been attempted previously, but always failed - building a database to catalog the hundreds of graphics in the small storage area. A dozen aisles of crates, 15 feet high and 50 feet long, it was a daunting feat. Thousands of square feet, holding countless posters, banners, backlit transparency films, foamcore signs, you name it.

I came up with a plan, but it wouldn't be quick or easy.

First I had the Top Men construction workers build a wall surrounding the whole storage area, enclosing it into its own room. This was necessary because sawdust from the construction area was always dirtying the graphics. That was particularly bad for backlit transparencies, because it was difficult to wipe off the sawdust without scratching or marring the surface.

After they built the room, I had them create big wooden placards to mount over each crate, at both ends of every aisle. In the graphic design department, I printed huge poster labels to attach on all the placards. Each row in the storage area was dubbed with a letter designation. Row A. Row B. Row C. Each crate had a number. Each bin on every crate had a letter.

So, for example, a graphic might be stored in Row D, Crate 9, Bin F.

That alone was a huge help in organizing the facility. But that wasn't good enough. You still had to know where a graphic was located or you'd spend hours hunting for it!

My solution?

I intended to label and photograph every single item in the storage bins and organize them in an image database on the computer. The database would have all the images tagged using keywords. Searches could be done in the computer via keywords to find any graphic within a few seconds. Simply type in some text appearing on the image, or describe the color or size, and all the images with those parameters would appear. The search results would tell you exactly what row, crate and bin the artwork was stored within. Having a corresponding label on the graphics meant you could easily return the graphic to its appropriate bin without having to use the computer to locate where it belonged.

These days, that would be a large job. Back in those days, it was even harder. At the time, digital photography was still in its infancy. Therefore, you couldn't find many computer programs which created image databases. I had to spend a lot of time doing research to find the best software.

The most ideal solution I discovered happened to only run on Apple computers.

No problem. There was an old Apple system in the office and I could just get that one running.

There was one small issue - the harddrive was dead. I needed $300 to get a new one.

It took me weeks to get the approval. The reason?

Because the president of Top Men, we'll call him Mr. Jerkhole, was a real jerkhole.

"Oh, the president of the company doesn't like Apple computers. Mr. Jerkhole wants you to do it on a Microsoft system."

... Excuse me?

A prime example of a bonehead who had no understanding of empowerment.

I've been a lifelong computer geek. I've owned many different computer systems. To me, computers are tools to get a job done, like a hammer or a screwdriver. I have no favoritism or prejudice against computers. Who cares?

Computers are just wrenches. I don't care if software runs on Apple or Microsoft or Linux or by the power of the freakin' tooth fairy! Get a life! Brands of hardware and formats of software are irrelevant. I just want to complete the work in the best way! I didn't care that the database solution I found only ran on Apple systems. I couldn't care less what computer it used. Just give me the tools I require!

Eventually, after a lot of pestering and walking into the presidents office to talk to him myself, I was finally able to procure a hard drive and get the storage and cataloging system up and running. Worked beautifully. Many of the old timer salesmen were overjoyed that they could come to me and request a graphic retrieval and I'd have it for them in 2 minutes, instead of 2 hours like it used to take. Even the moronic Mr. Jerkhole was impressed with the finished system.

No thanks to Mr. Jerkhole, I would have completed the project weeks earlier.

That was a big lesson for me in learning how frustrating a lack of empowerment can be. To move so far into a project, only to have some nitwit put up a brick wall, because of his irrational personal bias against a computer brand? Fool.

Ironically, I saw both ends of the spectrum regarding "empowerment" while working at another company.

The boss who understood the idea of empowerment, and who taught me the importance of empowerment, never allowed me to call him my "boss" and, in fact, was upset with me when I introduced him as such. It was none other than Mr. Cooldude, from the previous chapter.

I told you we worked at a very cool startup technology company. One weekend, I brought some friends to our studio to show off the facility. A renovated warehouse, the loft had towering ceilings and magnificent windows overlooking the city skyline. Like a superhero headquarters!

So, I brought my friends to the studio and Mr. Cooldude was there, painting his office. Like I said, we were a small startup and he owned the business, so it wasn't all that odd for the president to painting his own office.

"Oh, Mr. Cooldude!" I said, "I didn't know you were here. This is my friend Smurfabuggle." Or whatever the heck his name was. Anyway, I continued, "This is my boss, Mr. Cooldude."

Mr. Cooldude and Smurfabuggle shook hands and were very cordial and polite to one another.

Come that Monday morning, Mr. Cooldude called me into his office and explained, "Don't ever introduce me as your boss again."

"Huh?" I chuckled. I thought he was kidding.

"I'm serious." He explained.

"Well, Mr. Cooldude," I said, "Your name is on my paychecks. So, I don't know what else to call you."

He conceded and said, "True, but I'm not your boss. At this level we are business partners. I don't ever want you to see me as a boss or treat me that way. Understand?"

I did understand. And I appreciated it. And in that moment, I gained more respect for him than any boss, er... any "business partner" I ever had.

Mr. Cooldude explained to me that even in his past business ventures, he always empowered his employees and treated them as his equals and partners. There was no hierarchy in his companies. No bosses. No managers. Everyone was a peer. "This is your company too." He would explain. "You run this company. I don't do it by myself. You are responsible for the company. You help the company succeed. Without you, the company fails. You're not coming to this office to do *a job*. You're coming to run *your company*."

Such a subtle difference in terminology.

Yet the psychological effects are enormous.

Think about it.

It's not a job... It's *your* company.

Imagine if the people you work with started to view their responsibilities in that way.

I know what you're thinking. Instilling that kind of empowerment is easy in a startup. Simple to make a person feel irreplaceable when there are 3 people on staff. Far more difficult to convince employees they are so essential and indispensable in a company with thousands of workers.

Nevertheless, the idea remains true. Whether your company has 3 people or 30,000 people, every single employee runs that business. Every employee has a vested interest in the place being successful. You are not doing a job. You are running a company.

This backfired in a humorous story which Mr. Cooldude shared, about an engineering team, at a previous company, who made a major modification to a product feature without consulting him. Discovering the alteration in a meeting, Mr. Cooldude got upset and asked the engineers what they thought they were doing.

"You gave us permission to do this. You told us to make it the best we could and we didn't have to consult you on it." The nervous engineer defended.

In front of a room full of tech heads, Mr. Cooldude had to simply laugh it off and concede that the engineer was correct. He had indeed granted his teams that empowerment. He couldn't get upset about their changes now. He asked for it.

And sure enough, the engineers knew what they were doing, and their changes ended up making the product better.

Mr. Cooldude treated us the same way. I was trusted to make purchases and decide how to allocate resources all the time. Never had to ask. Never required permission. I just did what had to be done. Was a beautiful way to work! We accomplished a great deal in a very short period of time as a direct result of the freedom afforded to us.

Remember my story about Mr. Assfog the Fingerpainter or whatever the heck he was? Hey, man, he was in his office drawing pictures instead of working at building a business. Might as well have been fingerpainting.

Anyway, you recall when Mr. Cooldude went off to assist another startup company, we were temporarily left to deal with Mr. Assfog as our new president. When Mr. Assfog came on the scene, I was no longer empowered to make company purchases. I had to get them approved through the shroud of assfog and in turn, he'd request the item from the owners.

Whatever.

Okay, at one point, we needed to procure a portable computer system for our studio, in order to facilitate doing remote broadcasts for our video service. It was a very technically specific system and was a bit more expensive than a standard desktop or laptop computer.

A few days after I put in the request, Mr. Assfog calls me to his office all happy and excited. "I have some good news! Your computer was approved! So, you can buy it right away!"

Huh? *My* computer?

He acted like he was doing me a favor. No, no, no! This wasn't *my* computer. The computer wasn't some trivial personal expense. It was a vital piece of equipment for our business. Without it, we were literally unable to offer the services we were promoting to our customers! Dude, you aren't doing me a favor. We need this system in order to run the company! It would be like having a photography studio with no cameras, and needing "approval" to buy one.

Are you kidding me?!

"We opened a hair salon, but we don't have any scissors. Can we get approval to buy some?"

"No, just use your teeth."

Give me a break! "Approving" the purchase of that computer simply wasn't optional - it was a requirement.

Mr. Cooldude comprehended the notion of empowerment.

Mr. Assfog didn't have a clue.

Maybe I'm being harsh on Mr. Assfog though. Perhaps he couldn't help himself. Maybe he was just high on fingerpaint fumes.

NOT SUCKING SUGGESTION #3:

Learn to empower the people who look to you for leadership. Expect genuine nobility and chivalry among your employees. That may sound foolish and naive. Maybe even too old fashioned. The truth is, life is what you make of it and there can be more decent and moral people around you than you think. You just have to make sure your life is filled with people who possess ethics. That starts with empowering them to be that way.

THE BOTTOM LINE
(How does this advice translate into profits?)

Let people have some authority to make decisions. Trust their choices. Let them know their opinions matter. Thereby improving retention of quality people, which translates into increased profits.

CHAPTER FOUR

"Don't be afraid to get your hands dirty."

- Anonymous

Be willing to assist your teams. Get in there and do some work with them. Stimulate the process. Encourage. Help. Be part of the group. People have so much more respect for leaders when the leader proves they are part of the community. Care. Participate. Show a vested interest in connecting with your employees.

Back in the days before I was born, two men in Ohio founded a successful photography lab together. We'll call them Mr. Worthless and Mr. Nobleman. As the years went by and Mr. Nobleman had a family, he intended to pass down the business to his children and give his sons the opportunity to be a part of the lab.

Mr. Worthless refused.

Naturally, Mr. Nobleman was upset and decided to tell Mr. Worthless to go jump off a bridge. Mr. Nobleman sold his half of the company and started his own photography lab.

Like a Hollywood movie with a happy ending, Mr. Nobleman's business thrived while the business of Mr. Worthless faltered and failed. As the old saying goes, "When you live right, things happen right."

I had the honor of working for Mr. Nobleman in his lab. He was a much older gentleman and near to retirement by the time I met him. He was warm and friendly and grandfatherly. He moved kind of slow and always had a smile on his face.

One of the things I appreciated about Mr. Nobleman, a thing that I will never forget and always stood out to me - he would say "Good Morning" to literally every single employee in the lab, every single day. One should note, he had built a very respectable business for himself. Our building covered thousands of square feet and must have had over 100 employees. So, it wasn't a 30 second task to greet everyone. It took a decent amount of time. Mr. Nobleman would make his rounds and bid his greetings anyway. Even though the place was huge. Even though he was getting on in age and couldn't move so well. He still said good morning to everyone. Every morning. Without fail.

Now that is some admirable integrity. No single boss at any company I have ever known took the time to do that, except Mr. Nobleman. The man showed true character. He was sincerely grateful that you worked for him. He even gave out a $1000 Christmas Bonus to every single employee, every single year. Considering I was making under $15,000 a year at that time, a $1000 bonus was pretty huge.

Mr. Nobleman understood the concept of "getting your hands dirty" and he helped out. Just because he was an executive didn't make any work we did menial or below him. He rolled up his sleeves and got right in there with us.

I'll always admire him for that. Truly heroic gentleman.

As for a bad example of a boss who did not get his hands dirty? A prime example would be the experience at Generic Computer Company when the Vice President failed to do his job and I got blamed for his incompetence.

We had a little tradeshow coming up and as the graphic designer, I was tasked with creating brochures for the show. Once I finished them, I took them to the Vice President, we'll call him Mr. Monkeyarmpitfunk, to have the designs approved.

Mr. Monkeyarmpitfunk told me the designs were great, so I told him I'd proceed with getting them printed for the tradeshow.

"Oh, no." Mr. Monkeyarmpitfunk said. "Don't worry about that. I can look into having that done. You don't need to worry about the printing."

"Cool. Okay. That sounds great." Famous last words.

The tradeshow came around and we had no brochures.

The president of the company was apparently quite miffed about this fact. He was one of those sneaky people who would sidle and complain behind your back though, so I had no idea he was upset. Once I found out he was upset, I explained calmly that Mr. Monkeyarmpitfunk took the responsibility to get the brochures printed after I gave them to him for approval. I figured that was all I needed to say.

Instead of the president berating Mr. Monkeyarmpitfunk for failing to keep his word, I was later given an "evaluation" where I was threatened with being fired, because I "didn't follow through" with the task.

Mr. Monkeyarmpitfunk was in the room and I pointed at him and said, "But Mr. Monkeyarmpitfunk said he was going to get the printing done. I trusted he would follow through. I finished the brochures. They were completed on time. The fact they were not printed wasn't my fault. The moment Mr.

Monkeyarmpitfunk said he would take care of it, the printing was his responsibility."

Apparently, they didn't see it that way.

I was told I had to make sure tasks of that nature were completed.

Honestly? They were right. I never should have trusted Mr. Monkeyarmpitfunk. That experience taught me that some bosses won't get their hands dirty, even when they give you their word that they will do so. My own destiny is in my own hands. Never again would I permit the incompetence of others to reflect poorly upon me.

From then on, I follow up. From then on, I copy everyone in the office on emails, so everyone has it in writing what was being done, by whom, and when it was expected.

That was a very infuriating and frustrating experience. Let's end this chapter on a much more positive note and a much nicer tale about bosses who get their hands dirty.

While working a really great position, at a Respectable Corporation in the Midwest, our division once had a number of layoffs. Always a sad and upsetting moment to experience, even though I was "one of the lucky ones" who remained gainfully employed.

During that time, the executives did something amazing though.

The president sent out an email, announcing none of the upper management were taking salary increases that year. Collectively, they decided, in light of eliminating so many salaries, it wasn't right to allow themselves to make more money. Total superhero virtues.

I was shocked. I was impressed. Who does that?

I mean, sure, I've done that myself at companies - offered to accept a lower salary, if it helps others to keep their jobs. But executives in a major corporation doing the same thing!? No way. That was unheard of.

That instant, learning these people had such decency, truly made me proud to be associated with ladies and gentlemen of such genuinely upstanding character and moral fiber.

What was my response? I was so bedazzled with their integrity, I sent out an email to the president and my teammates, offering to do the same thing - to eschew a salary increase - and suggesting to my peers that they consider following suit.

That little stunt did not go over very well with my manager. I got a little "talking to" and was told that my email was inappropriate and I can not do that sort of thing.

Oh, really?

I told her it was morally the right thing to do and I would do it again.

Thankfully, the president found my email to be admirable and forwarded it to all of the executives! Pretty cool. I certainly wasn't expecting that.

In the end, all of us grunts still got our yearly pay raise. While a pay raise for an executive was substantial, I guess my increase was too paltry to matter in the grand scheme of such a large company. But, that's not the point. The point is - we're all in this together. Getting your hands dirty can also mean making a sacrifice, not only as a boss or a manager, but as a fellow human being, no matter where you are on that totem pole.

NOT SUCKING SUGGESTION #4:

Getting your hands dirty can mean many things. Mostly, it simply means helping out your fellow employees when you can. When you give your word to do something, see it done. When the finances are in turmoil, look to make some sacrifices to your own salary before throwing people out into the street. Turn a wrench. Serve a meal. Whatever your business does, roll up your sleeves and work alongside your teams on occasion. Sure beats going to another meeting.

THE BOTTOM LINE

(How does this advice translate into profits?)

Assisting your personnel and being "one of the boys" on the frontlines will help get a lot more work done. Thereby improving efficiency, which translates into increased profits.

CHAPTER FIVE

"A suspicious parent makes an artful child."

- Anonymous

In psychology, "projection" is the act of applying your own personality to that of other people. Therefore, a person who steals is going to presume others are thieves. Someone who lies all the time will think everyone else is dishonest. Folks who are decent and lawful will imagine fellow citizens are equally upstanding and good. You get the idea. Beyond the way we perceive others, we also behave as we are treated. Regard your employees as trustworthy and they will tend to be exactly that. Consider employees to be slackers and they will likely be slothful.

Supposedly, the original meaning of the opening quote in this chapter was intended to convey the notion that the more parents push their children to excel, the more the child will achieve.

I never took it that way.

To me, that quote has always meant, "If you don't trust your kid, you'll just teach them to be a sneaky little devil."

Employers are very lucky when you decide to work for them and contribute to the company.

Think about all you are giving them. Your talents. Your skills. Your experience. Most of all, you are giving the most valuable and precious gift that every human being on this earth possesses - time. We only have a short number of days upon this beautiful earth. Every second you give to your job is a sacred moment in time you could be spending with someone you love. You could spend that time with your children. On a beach. Talking to your grandparents. Laughing with your friends. Any number of precious experiences could be enriching your life during your workday time.

But, no.

Instead, you're at work.

Therefore, your boss is incomprehensibly privileged to have you. Any business on earth should be honored that you would share your time with them.

Once upon a time, a boss explained to me that people behave the way they are treated. Show an employee trust and she will be trustworthy. Offer an employee a salary larger than they expect and they will feel compelled to earn that income. Give an employee time off, without question, and they will be more apt to return as fast as possible. Grant an open policy to let people slack off and surf the Internet at work, and they'll waste far less time doing it than they would if it was forbidden.

We all know these things to be true.

Think about the bosses you have had who micro-managed every move you made and were constantly looking over your shoulder. Did you work hard for those people?

No.

You resented them for continually hassling you, so you did as little work as possible, just to spite them. If they didn't trust you, why should you do what they asked? They are going to treat you like a steamy pile of elephant crap anyway. So you only did what you had to do to get by. No point in going the extra mile for those featherbrains. Right?

Indeed.

(Yes, I know you used far more colorful language than "featherbrain" to describe them. Listen, I'm trying to keep this book tasteful enough so your spouse doesn't kill you when your 6 year old decides to read it, because they see the cover and think it's a comic book. Okay?)

The boss who told me, "People behave the way they are treated", was correct.

Like the Internet issue.

He told me, "People who work in an office are going to surf around on the Internet at work. If you yell at people for it, they won't stop. They'll just get stressed out and sneaky about it. If you let people do it, then they will be more productive, because they won't feel the temptation to be deceptive or secretive. Treat people like they are slacking off, and they will. Treat people like they are getting the work done, and they will."

Wise fellow.

The salary lesson was a big one too. His philosophy was so simple it blew my mind. His attitude was pure genius. The thing about paying people more than they expect produces astounding results. Never before or since have I seen any company pontificating that sort of philosophy. When he explained it to me, the brilliant ingenuity behind that philosophy became unquestionable. For example, he said he'd always pay about 5% above whatever salary range a person expected. If someone interviews for a position and asks for $35,000 he will offer them $37,000.

Why?

Simple psychology - it makes an employee feel they are truly valued. Instead of walking into a company and having to negotiate a salary and fighting with a finance department which is attempting to give you the least amount of money you are willing to take, he gives you more. Not a lot more. Just a little.

Genius.

Of course, 99% of companies in the world would never dream of doing that. They want to hire you for the lowest price possible. Why?

They think that is smart for their "bottom line" but they fail to see the long-term damage of that mentality.

Hiring employees for the lowest salary they are willing to settle for, sends a message to the employee that the company doesn't value them. The company is saying, "We barely think you're worth this much."

Now, weight the psychological effect of that message against the apathy of the typical employee. Think about how much people slack off at work. Think about how much money a company loses each year, from each employee, simply because that employee doesn't give their job 100%.

Can you blame the employee? Why should they give 100% to their job? Right out of the gate, the company hired that employee for the minimum amount of money they were willing to accept. Why should an employee give 100% to their job when the company tried to underpay them from the start?

I know. I know. I spoke earlier about nobility and chivalry and it's not noble or righteous to agree to a lower salary and then use that as an excuse to slack off. If you agree to the compensation, you should give your 100%. Right? No one forced you to accept the position, so you shouldn't complain.

I get that.

I agree.

But we're not talking about they way people *should* behave. We're talking about the way people *do* behave. And I'm telling you - if an employee feels intimidated to accept a lowball salary, versus an employee who is offered more than they are asking, you will see a huge difference in attitude, simply because of they way they were treated.

Underpay employees from the moment you hire them and I guarantee the apathy it instills will cost the company more than 5% worth of productivity every year. Easily.

Now imagine the loyalty and work ethic you can instill in people by offering them even more than they asked for.

When you see an expected salary range of $40,000 to $50,000 on a resume, offer the job for $53,000. Watch and see the reaction you'll get. Your company will easily earn that extra $3000 back, in increased productivity, in no time flat.

People behave the way they are treated.

Treat your employees like cheap and expendable parts in a machine, and that is exactly how they will perform.

Treat your employees like priceless and valuable individuals with a lot of unique talents and skills to contribute, and that is exactly what they will be.

One of the best personal examples of that? There was a day I was working a job when there happened to be some amazing weather conditions for hang gliding. Any surfer can relate to that feeling. When the swell rolls in and the waves are breaking, you can't be in an office. You have to be at the beach. Same thing applies when you're a hang glider pilot.

I was at work for about 5 minutes before I walked into my bosses office and asked him if I could take the day off to go flying.

He laughed and rolled his eyes (he knew me pretty well by that point). He asked if I could still get my latest project done by Friday if I took today off. Sure! Just work a few 10 hour days and I'll be able to crank it out, no problem.

He was cool with it.

So, I split and went soaring in the sky for the remainder of the day.

I put in some extra hours and got the project done on time, just like he asked. Just like I promised.

People behave the way they are treated. He was respectful and considerate of my time, therefore I was willing to devote the time he requested in return. Everyone is happy. I got my hang gliding flights and he got his project finished by our deadline.

An example of the opposite?

I was working a different job when my grandfather passed away. I got the phonecall at work. I was smack dab in the middle of a project, but that was no longer relevant. I set down the things I was working on and walked into my managers office and said, "My grandfather died. I'm going home. I'm not sure when I'll be back."

I went home and that was that.

I recall my mother saying to me, "That's really nice that they let you take off work."

"What?" I laughed. "What are you talking about? Grandpa died. I didn't ask for permission to leave work. I told them I'm going home. No boss will ever have the authority to tell me what to do in a situation like that. Family comes first. Period."

But wouldn't you know, 5 days later, I got a phonecall from the company asking me when I planned on coming back to the office.

Excuse me? My grandfather dies and in less than a week and they were already pestering me? Honestly, I had intended on going back to work in another day or two. Instead, I waited 3 more days out of spite.

People behave the way they are treated.

Up to you. Want to treat your employees like criminals or superheroes?

Let someone leave work to go hang gliding, or surfing, or take their friend to the airport, and they will show extra loyalty right back.

Pester someone after a death in the family, or because they have to take their kid to the doctor, and you'll be lucky if they come back to work at all.

NOT SUCKING SUGGESTION #5:

Don't simply "treat people the way you want to be treated", like the old saying goes. This is deeper than that. This is realizing that the way you treat people will actually influence their behavior. Just like children are impressionable and can be manipulated to act the way you want, the same applies to adults. That's not meant to be as insidious or sinister as it sounds. Being "manipulative" is not always a bad thing. You have the power to manipulate people in positive ways. Utilize that power. Treat people the way you want them to behave. If you want honest, hardworking personnel, then treat them as though that is what they already are.

KAPOW!

THE BOTTOM LINE
(How does this advice translate into profits?)

People have very mailable personalities and can be easily influenced to behave poorly or to behave well. Show your employees trust and give them a sense of value. Thereby improving retention of quality people, which translates into increased profits.

CHAPTER SIX

"Failure is not an option."

- Anonymous

Recognize that people have more than a single skillset and utilize it. See beyond the job you hired them to perform. Too many companies treat their teammates like robots that can only perform one task. The truth is, people are exceptionally diverse and multifaceted and many of them can perform world-class work in multiple roles. Discover their talents. Give them the opportunity to showcase their other abilities.

Personally, I would have loved to have worked for good old Walt Disney. He was the one man in business that I respect and admire enough to just do what he thought was best, without question. Sadly, I never met the guy. Heck, he passed away before I was even born. (I know I already mentioned that in the dedication, but, let's face it, how many people ever actually read those?) But I'd work for him.

There are many well documented stories about Walt moving people into different jobs around the Studio, simply because he felt they would excel at them. Especially during the time when he founded WED Enterprises to build Disneyland, he would pull people out of their field into an entirely new position. They would kick and scream and complain and say, "Walt, why are you assigning me to this?! I don't know anything about this type of work!"

Walt would believe in them, and reassure them, and sure enough, they'd stick with it, and they would soar.

Can you imagine a boss who not only values what you are worth, but cares enough to recognize skills you don't even realize you have?

Yes, I would have loved to have worked for Walt Disney.

Everyone else on earth is someone I work *with* and not someone I work *for*.

Walt tells a story that when he moved to California and was looking to get into the motion picture business, he would have been willing to sweep floors, just to get his foot in the door.

Definitely the proper attitude for Tinseltown.

There's an old saying about success in Hollywood - "It's not what you know, it's *who* you know."

Starry-eyed wanna-bes who just fell off the turnip truck actually think that phrase is true.

It's a lie.

Those of us who have made a living in Hollywood know the real deal - "It's not who you know, it's who knows *you*."

You can "network" and "name drop" all you want in Los Angeles. The people you meet, the folks you think you know, are not relevant to your success. What matters is, who knows *you*? Who thinks *you* are talented? Who finds *you* to be an asset? Who knows *your* name? Because if that list of people is worthless, you best just turn around and get right back on the next turnip truck headed home.

There can be no fallback plan.

Failure is not an option.

Thanks to being known unto a good friend who happens to be a successful cinematographer, my first job in California was actually pretty cool. I was hired as a graphic designer at a startup company in Hollywood. We'll call the company The California Dream. Located in a penthouse highrise, I was developing an innovative trivia gaming system that ran on home video players. Quite an exciting venture, the project required knowledge of movies, video editing, graphic design, programming and creative brainstorming. While there, I conceptualized and built an entire feature of the game system on my own. Was really cool to see it fully functional in the final production product, knowing it was totally my construct. An impressive environment, I had a fantastic view of the city out my office windows and could watch the skyline of Hollywood sparkle to light after every sunset.

Totally awesome. Fantastic place to work.

Also happened to be the first job I was laid-off from in Los Angeles.

When they gave me the boot, the buttclown owner of the company who hired me in the first place didn't have the courage to can me herself - she had her patsy president do it - some wealthy, unkempt hipster with an electric SUV. Don't even recall his name. They also tried to screw me out of the unemployment checks I was legally entitled to collect. Real class act, those losers.

So, anyway, the owner, Ms. Buttclown, suffered from an ailment that many people have and is an epidemic rampant in the corporate universe. Namely, she was incapable of recognizing any skills a person might possess outside of their job description.

Walt Disney she was not.

I have been a professional cinematographer, a professional video editor, a professional computer programmer, and a professional graphic designer. By "professional" I mean I actually got paid enough while working in those fields to cover the rent and keep food on the table. Additionally, as a photographer, I've had my photography shown and sold in art galleries all over the country. As a filmmaker, I had an award-nominated short film which I wrote and directed shown in multiple film festivals around the country too. I'm a published novelist, published as a short story author, and now I can add being an author of business book to that list.

In other words, when someone hires me 9-to-5 as a graphic designer, they are getting someone with the capability to contribute far more to the company than my job description.

We had a kid at The California Dream who did all our video editing. We'll call him Mr. Fartknocker. He claimed to be an award-winning filmmaker who won a million-dollar best-picture prize in a film festival for his movie. We came to find out later, the festival he entered was a sham, and the curators absconded with all the entry fees, and none of the "winners" ever collected a dime. In other words, Mr. Fartknocker bragged about winning a film festival scam that never awarded a single thing.

Ah, only in Hollywood.

In the rest of the world, it would be embarrassing to "win" a film festival that was a lie.

In Hollywood, boneheads are so desperate for acceptance, they even consider illegitimate accolades to be bragging rights.

Anyhow, around Christmas time, Mr. Fartknocker went back to wherever Podunk wheat-field he was from, to see family. Morontown, Idaho or something.

We had a big section of the game to edit and Mr. Fartknocker was gone for 3 weeks or something. At that time, I had already edited multiple music videos, educational films, a feature-length movie, my award-nominated short-film, and numerous corporate videos. In other words, as an editor, I had a heck of a lot more experience than Mr. Fartknocker Who Won A Million Phony Dollars.

Naturally, I volunteered to help out and do all the required video editing while Mr. Fartknocker was back home in Stupidville.

Ms. Buttclown was reluctant, because I was a graphic designer after all. What did I know about editing?

Ugh.

So, anyway, Ms. Buttclown eventually rescinds and lets me edit the project and it turns out great. Ms. Buttclown and I work closely with one another for 3 solid weeks. Ms. Buttclown offers her input. I make changes. I tweak the edits. I get it all functioning exactly the way she wants it. I'm stoked because I know this whole experience is giving me a fantastic opportunity to prove my worth and showcase my diversity and make me a stronger asset to the company. Working one-on-one with the president and exceeding her expectations is just awesome! Everything goes off without a hitch and I'm getting compliments on my work. Rad.

Sometime in March, a mere 3 months later, our naive little video editor, Mr. Fartknocker had to go back to Backwater, Nebraska again. Once more, we'd be without an editor.

No problem. I had already proven myself 3 months ago on the huge project. Again, I offered to assist.

The president of the company, Ms. Buttclown, with whom I had edited video on a daily basis for nearly a month, looks at me and says, "Oh? Eric, you don't know how to edit video, do you?"

I laughed, because I thought she was joking.

Gradually, I realized... she was serious.

Ouch. They say, "Scars are tattoos with better stories." That left a scar.

I was crushed. All that work, all that time spent proving myself and showing off my diversity, wasted. Ms. Buttclown couldn't see me as anything but a graphic designer. That is what she hired me for. That is all I was. No matter that I

77

worked with her everyday for 3 weeks as an editor. She forgot all about that. Because... well, I honestly don't know the "because"... because she was a knucklehead?

(Again, I'm just trying to be gracious. Trust me, I had far more unseemly terms for her than "knucklehead" too. Most of the phrases implicated her in lewd acts involving farm animals or parental figures.)

The strange thing is, years later, I found myself working at a large corporation where a number of people actually did appreciate my diversity. Although I was brought on board as a developer and programmer, I was given opportunities to do things like photography for some of our large corporate events, video editing for special projects, and graphic design for others. Two ends of the spectrum - a small startup and a massive corporation - and each worked out with the opposite results you'd expect.

The little startup didn't appreciate my diversity and treated me like a machine.

The big corporation recognized my talents and gave me various opportunities.

Wait. Let me rephrase that. The big corporation recognized my *experience*. Not talents. I find it obnoxious when people regard themselves as having "talent" at anything. Others can say one is "talented" - saying it about oneself is just arrogant. I have learned "skills" and "experiences" but I can't call my abilities "talent" without sounding like, well, Mr. Fartknocker.

Let me interject another important idea here and this applies to both bosses and employees - STOP THINKING OF YOUR JOB AS YOUR JOB DESCRIPTION!

It's not.

Your job is your *time*.

Got it?

Your job is *not* about your hired skill. It is an investment of your time. That is what you bring to the table. Time.

I always view jobs that way. I was hired as a whole person - a complete being with various abilities I can contribute to an organization.

I'm not a machine.

I'm not a robot designed to do a singular task.

I am there to share *all* my potential skills during a designated time.

Remember the previous chapter where I talked about giving your time to a job? Start viewing life that way. Don't walk through the doors every morning with a "that's not my job" mentality. Contribute *all* your knowledge and skills to your position. If you have a capability to assist, then help out. Even if it goes outside of your job description. Remember, this is *your* company. You want to keep paying that rent and sending those kids to school, start acting like this is your *company* and not just your *job*. When you approach the job as your own company, your whole outlook changes. Suddenly, you won't hesitate to do whatever needs to be done to get the place running smoothly. Even if it means doing something outside the realm of what your were "hired to do" in the first place.

Be careful with that mentality though.

Apparently some lazy people don't appreciate it.

I once worked a movie set where the catering crew was setting up food in the dark, in a public reception hall. I flicked the lightswitch on the wall and said, "Why don't you guys turn the lights on?"

I got yelled at because, "Only one of the electrician guys can turn on the lights."

Like so many of my stories involving workplace idiocy, I thought they were joking. They weren't.

"Excuse me?" I said. "This isn't a film studio lighting rig. I mean, if it were a professional light on the film set, I can understand that. But this is just an ordinary lightswitch on the wall of a church reception hall!"

"Still," the catering dude said. "Only a crew electrician is allowed to turn that on. You're not supposed to touch it."

Wow.

People become so blinded by job descriptions they literally can't turn on a lightbulb?!

I scoffed, "If any electrician honestly thinks flipping on a household lightswitch is a job skill, that person doesn't deserve a job."

Seriously. Turn on the damn lights. Don't wait for someone else to do it for you. Don't be a fartknocking buttclown. Help out. Go above and beyond what is expected of you.

Speaking of Fartknocker and Buttclown, the truth is, I'm really grateful to Ms. Buttclown. She gave me my first Hollywood job. After years of dreaming about living in Los Angeles, I had finally made it and she gave me my first real opportunity to make something of myself in this town. The job was genuinely fun and exciting. I had a great time doing it. I learned a lot of new graphic arts skills and honed my abilities. We had a blast doing big testing parties on the games. It was a truly wonderful experience.

Honestly, even the fact they eventually tried to cheat me out of my unemployment benefits was something I can count as a beneficial experience. It taught me a lot of diligence into researching laws. As a result, I educated myself a great deal on where to find legal information and how to discover the correct documents and build a solid legal defense against unfair claims. All in all, a lot of good came out of it. Too bad I was still awarded my benefits and outsmarted Ms. Buttclown in court, considering her first profession was a lawyer.

Hm. Never thought of that before. Maybe she couldn't acknowledge my other skills because she sucked at her own primary profession!

I especially enjoyed showing up that pansy president. That felt particularly gratifying. Take a bath, you hipster!

NOT SUCKING SUGGESTION #6:

Remember that people are working with you. Never for you. This isn't medieval Europe. You're not a king. Employees are not surfs or simpletons. They all have a wide range of skills that you can use in your business. Even if their skills seem unrelated to anything your company is doing, take the time to learn about what they can do. Maybe an employee who restores old cars can help your clothing company because they have done a lot of research on the Internet to find parts, just like you look for rare fabrics. Maybe a person who has a model airplane hobby and is familiar with the laws about flying them can assist your non-profit homeless shelter because they know many other laws regarding legal rights. Things that seem totally different from the needs of your company may prove to be of priceless importance.

THE BOTTOM LINE

(How does this advice translate into profits?)

Instead of hiring people for singular skillset, look to see the versatility of people in your organization. Having them assist in more than one role eliminates them getting burned out on one task. Thereby improving efficiency, which translates into increased profits.

CHAPTER SEVEN

"People will forget when a movie was released. They will always remember if it was good."

- Anonymous

Deadlines should be met, but far often, meeting them is less important than doing outstanding work. This is not to say deadlines are irrelevant. Sometimes a deadline is a "necessary evil" and must be achieved. In the medical profession, failing to meet a deadline could mean life or death. For most of the working world, missing the deadline won't kill anyone. Make all your work fantastic. Never slack. Never cut corners. Bad work will never be forgotten. Late work will usually be forgiven.

Dumb saying. "The watched pot never boils." Watched pots do boil. Of course they do! But when the pot is an employee who feels overworked, it usually gives you the finger when you turn your back.

Flex time is a notion that is lost on most of the Western world.

For those who don't know what "flex time" is and what it means - it is the idea that your time is flexible and you work when you want. If you are a person who earns a salary for working 40 hours a week, you still work 40 hours a week. You just don't have to clock those hours from 9-to-5 from Monday through Friday. You can fulfill your 40 hours a week in any combination of hours you wish. Work 4 days for 10 hours each. Work 7 days a week for 6 hours a day. Whatever you desire. That is flex time.

Naturally, flex time is not an option for all businesses. Most retail businesses for example, are obligated to be open during their posted hours. But, for those companies where it is a possibility (or even for select and befitting personnel within a company), it should always be encouraged.

For the lucky few, flex time also constitutes working to finish projects, not to fulfill an obligation of certain hours on the clock. If you are designated 40 hours to finish a job and you have it done in 25, you can take a day or two off. That version of "flex time" is a rarity, but it's another way the term is applied.

Remember chapter five? People behave the way they are treated.

Many companies and bosses fear that flex time will be abused. They imagine people will take advantage of the flexibility and only show up to work for 5 hours a day. In practice, I've found exactly the opposite to be the case. Typically, people will work well over 8 hours a day when you tell them, "I don't care what hours you work, just get the work finished by this date."

For many years, I was locked into the 9-to-5 mentality like most people. Just like you, I was afraid to be late. I was trapped like a mindless lemming in that zombie state of clockwatching like everyone else.

All that changed when I was working at a company with the person who introduced me to flex time. I was building a website and I had some code I needed to use, but it was saved on a computer back at home.

I commented to the boss, "I can't build this right now, but I'll go get the code when I go home for lunch."

He sighed and looked at me, "Eric, do you really need that to do your job?"

"Yes."

"Then go get it," he said. "You don't need to wait for lunch. If you have to go home now, just go home. You're going to learn, I'm not watching the clock, trying to see how much time you spend sitting at your desk. I don't care how long you are at your desk. I care about you getting the work finished. I want you to get your work done. Whatever you need to do to make that happen, just do it."

I was kind of shocked. Part of the reason I was shocked was because I had no idea he'd be such a cool person. I never expected such a reaction.

The other mindblowing thing was how simple and logical his attitude was about finishing the work. As soon as the words left his mouth, I was stunned that everyone didn't think this way. This is the attitude all bosses should have, I thought!

"Oh. Okay. Cool." I responded.

So I left. I went home and got what I needed.

And an amazing thing happened - I didn't slack off. Once I was given that freedom, once I was trusted with that flexibility, I didn't waste my time. In fact, I really made sure I had some hustle and urgency and returned to the office in a timely manner.

Why?

Because I felt like I owed it to him.

He wasn't being some distrustful micro-managing jerk. He gave me total freedom and I felt obligated to honor that.

Personally, there are three rules I strive to abide in all my work:

1. Do everything with the best possible quality and integrity. Never slack off. Never cut corners. Make sure everything is done to the edge of my capability. World class. Top notch. All the time. No excuses. With every task, I am building a legacy and reputation for my own work ethic. Best to keep it classy.

2. Do that work as quickly as possible. Don't drag my feet or procrastinate. Get it done. Now.

3. Learn as many new skills along the way as possible.

That's it. Pretty simple.

No one taught me those rules. I was never schooled on them. Never learned those rules from a book or at a seminar. Those rules simply manifested themselves organically, as self-evident truths, after years of experience in the work-a-day world. Those chart-happy nincompoops blowing a bunch of assfog like, well, Mr. Assfog, would do well to learn those three philosophies.

You see, if everyone followed those rules, from the top on down, there would be no need for the mindless meetings and the useless pyramid charts. People would be working. Accomplishing things. Learning. Improving. Innovating.

That was why I didn't slack off when I was given the freedom to go home to get the code I required.

Shortly after publishing my first novel, I found myself working in the digital graphics department at a professional photography lab. The manager there was one of those "clockwatcher" types. When you were 5 minutes late to work, he'd let you know.

Don't ask me why, but I had awful luck being on time to that job. Maybe it was the 40 minute commute. Maybe it was Fate. Maybe it was Karma. Maybe it was simply an alien conspiracy involving spacetime experiments. Who knows? All I know is, I was about 10 minutes late no matter what I did. Every single day. All the time. I even tried setting my alarm 30 minutes earlier and I still got in the darn office at 9:10 every day. So frustrating.

Now, I should note that according to state law, legally, we were also permitted two 10 minute breaks during each work day. That's a total of 20 minutes a day that we were expected to not work. Two breaks which I never took advantage of, I might add. Not once. I always worked through my breaks.

One day, Mr. Clockwatcher pulls me aside to "talk" with me. He complains about the fact that I'm late every single day.

He was right. I couldn't deny it. I couldn't argue the point. I was late. I wasn't happy about it either. Made me feel like a slacker and I wasn't.

However, in my defense, I pointed out the fact I never took breaks. "Since we are allowed 20 minutes a day and I never take those breaks," I said, "then even though I may be 10 minutes late, by the end of the week, I'm still working 50 minutes longer than everyone else."

Mr. Clockwatcher laughed at me and said, "Well, no, it doesn't work that way."

Oh?

What? What pray tell doesn't work what way?

What are you talking about?!

Apparently, in Mr. Clockwatcher Dreamland, mathematics worked differently! Who knew?

I'm not sure why math "doesn't work that way" in his brain, but that was his problem, not mine. I was in the backroom of a photography lab and I was always ahead of schedule on my jobs. I never interact with customers and customers wouldn't be showing up for another hour anyway! Who cares if I'm 10 minutes late?

I became increasingly livid each time I replayed the conversation in my head.

Yes, I was "in the wrong" and I should be on time.

I won't deny that.

But why was I not given credit for the extra work I did?

Did he appreciate that I literally worked longer than anyone else?

No.

Did he care that every project I did was always completed in time for the customer to pick it up?

No.

He just complained that I wasn't there when *he* expected.

He didn't care about the quantity or the quality of work I completed. He only cared about *when* the work was performed.

Being punctual is important when your job is time-sensitive. If you're a doctor, you better be in that emergency room on time. If you're a lawyer, you need to defend your client and show up at the court when expected. If you run a bank, you have a legal obligation to open when scheduled.

But, let's face it, most of us are not curing any terminal diseases. Thanks to technology, many white collar workers can now work remotely and log into their business computers from home or from a laptop at the beach. The concept of working during specific hours has become rather obsolete in some professions. Important back in the 20th century, perhaps, but not as applicable in the modern world.

I know. I know.

It's not working.

No matter what I say, you're still not convinced. You still think "flex time" and "show up when you want" translates into "lazy slackers not doing their job" and you won't stand for it. You think I'm full of it.

Fair enough. I don't blame you.

You are right - people can too easily take advantage of it.

Okay, if you insist I'm wrong, here is my suggestion - try it temporarily. If you don't trust that flex time will work, make it a temporary change in your organization or on your team. Offer them true flex time for a week or two. Lay out the ground rules and see what happens.

If they abuse the privilege, you can easily discontinue the practice.

Try it. Experiment.

If you are lucky enough to already have flex time in your organization, treat the opportunity with respect. Work in a way that will maximize your productivity.

The old "work smarter, not harder" adage is one of my favorites. In fact, it's almost a prerequisite philosophy in order for flex time to be effective. You must be very intelligent about the way you allocate your time.

"Hard work" is often regarded as a noble thing. Frequently, "hard work" *is* a noble thing. But just as important is working intelligently.

Truth is, hard work can be a foolhardy thing if done while blind to an understanding of the task. Hard work without a comprehensive purpose can often lead to unnecessary labor being performed. When you truly understand *why* you are being asked to complete a job, you will always be able to engage in that work far more efficiently.

Bosses rarely allow that.

Question the motives and too many bosses will tell you, "Just get it done!"

Well, if the Mr. Turdbrain barking orders tells you *why* everyone is doing a mad dash to get this project finished, perhaps you can offer suggestions which would give the same results in one third the time, without forcing 15 people to work overtime. When a boss practices the notion of "transparency" and shares the "what and why" behind an endeavor, the team is better informed and can achieve things much more quickly, simply by bringing to bear more of their intelligence and experience.

Your people are bright. Treat them as such.

Work smarter. Not harder.

NOT SUCKING SUGGESTION #7:

Allow flex time and realize that quality is usually far more essential than meeting deadlines. Don't ignore deadlines. They are still important. Just make sure people are working smart and utilizing their time in the best and most efficient way possible for them and their lives. Encourage your teams to "work smarter, not harder" and find creative solutions to difficult problems. Watch the quality, not the clock.

THE BOTTOM LINE
(How does this advice translate into profits?)

Working without feeling oppressed and shackled will make people work harder and with less stress. Thereby improving efficiency, which translates into increased profits.

CHAPTER EIGHT

"You catch more bees with honey than vinegar."

- Anonymous

This is an old concept and it bears repeating in every single managerial advice book. Why? Because the boss still doesn't take the time to do it! Praise people. Let them know they are doing a good job. Tell them you are impressed. Simple compliments can change everything about someone's attitude. Cater to their ego. Make them feel awesome and they will perform awesome. For goodness sake, don't ever be phony in your compliments. The praise has to be sincere. Phony praise is worse than keeping your mouth shut. Mean what you say.

Have you ever been to Disneyland? If you haven't, you absolutely must spend a day there before you depart this lovely planet.

Disneyland truly is The Happiest Place on Earth. For those who have never been there, you might doubt that. Cynicism seems to be so in vogue among our culture these days, many folks doubt bright and joyful things as being real.

My first trip to Disneyland, I learned something wonderful that I never realized until I went there. The reason Disneyland is The Happiest Place on Earth is because the Cast Members are genuine and sincere. I've visited Disneyland many times over the years and I've seen the most cynical of brooding teenagers turn into giddy children again. I knew one man who told me his agoraphobic wife began to overcome her agoraphobia by making repeat visits to the park.

Why is it such a magical place?

Sincerity.

Plain and simple.

The Cast Members treat guests with honest respect and courtesy. There is nothing false or phony about it. The smiles, the attitude, the demeanor is all from the heart. As a result, that joy and sincerity become contagious. People end up bringing out the best in each other.

That is also the key to complimenting people in the workplace.

Being sincere.

Sorry.

I know I got you dreaming about Disneyland and then I sucked you back into the workplace thing. Forgive me. It was a dirty trick.

But, I'm serious about *sincerity* being the key to really making people feel good and boosting morale.

One of the best compliments I ever got at a job was from a person I couldn't stand. We didn't get along.

Not sure if you can tell from reading this far, but I can sometimes be a bit... (ahem) abrasive? Caustic, perhaps? Yeah.

I don't mean to be! Honestly, if you met me in person, you'd find I'm a rather chipper and upbeat fellow most of the time! I doubt I've given that impression, considering the tone of this book, but I am fairly full of cheerful smiles and friendly laughter. I'm just very blunt about things and have little patience for people who take pride in ignorance. When I think something is stupid, I have no problem saying, "That's dumb. What are you thinking?"

That's not a personal attack. Doing something moronic and *being* a moron are entirely different things. The brightest of folks can all be dunces on occasion.

Rumor has it, even I make mistakes from time to time... Doubtful. But that's what I hear.

Joking aside, people who are really sensitive don't differentiate between those things too well - being an idiot versus doing something idiotic. They never react well to being told an action is dumb. They get all butthurt and whine and stuff. They take it all personally.

So, during an afternoon many years ago, one of those easily-butthurt people got all confrontational with me because they felt I was being "mean" or something. Instead of feeling guilty and apologetic, I just thought, "What is this, high school?"

Anyway, many weeks later, that same person overheard I was interested in taking some graphic design classes at the local community college. "Why would you waste your time with that?" He asked. "I teach classes at that school and you already know more than any of the faculty on staff. Taking classes there would be a waste of your time. They can't teach you anything you don't already know."

Holy cow.

Talk about being made to feel like a superhero!

Suddenly I felt guilty for all those snotty things I had been thinking! What a nice thing to say.

That one compliment, that one phrase, made all the difference in the world to me. Suddenly, I wanted to treat this fella differently. I wanted to make an extra effort to do good work. I wanted to be more sensitive to his feelings and not be so snarky. In a nutshell, I wanted to not only live up to the expectations I was viewed with, but to exceed them.

All that from one compliment.

Many people are like that. Your own employees are like that. Take them aside and tell them something special. Notice something they have done. Don't just say, "Good job, Joe."

No. This is more than that. Trite compliments are practically insults. Don't do that. Remember Disneyland. It can't be phony. It must be honest. Give good old Joe a heartfelt compliment.

Tell Joe something like, "I like giving you the drywall installations because you do them better than anyone else on the team."

Be specific. Let people know that you pay attention to their work. You notice. You appreciate their talents.

One word. One sentence. One compliment. You'll be shocked how much that alone will boost morale.

I had one employer promote me and give me a $10,000 raise and tell me I was "The Golden Child" for the company. Never forgot that. What an amazing thing to be told. Praise like that makes people do a lot more work. Makes people devote far more effort into their tasks. In fact, I regularly worked 12 and 14 hour days at that job. Not because I had to. Not because I was threatened with losing my job. Not because I was earning overtime (because I wasn't). No. I worked 14 hour days because I loved to do it. Because the president of the company instilled me with empowerment, with a sense of ownership, with a vested interest in our success, and with a feeling of importance.

That was *my* company.

That was *my* studio.

So I devoted tons of time to it.

Treating me with respect and praising me, so that I had a sense of worth and value, really worked. It was effective. It made me work my butt off.

You know what never works?

You know what never boosts morale?

Being ignored. Being unappreciated.

Morale vanishes when you work hard, when you invent ways to improve the company, when you go above and beyond your job duties, and no one cares. No one notices. No one gives a damn.

That makes very gifted people pick up and leave jobs.

Another great way to eliminate all loyalty and morale? Being threatened with being fired.

Or as sucky bosses like to say, "If the situation doesn't improve, we may have to scale things back."

A favorite euphemism for, "You better impress us or you're fired."

That is what is truly being said.

"We have to like you, or you're getting the boot."

That never makes anyone want to work harder. That just makes people angry and resentful. Bitter. Furious. Some experts in human behavior even note that such threats can often make people slack off and do a worse job. By implanting the fear of losing a job, people get so stressed, their performance drops. (No, I don't have a reference to the research. I know I read it somewhere. Just go on the Internet and look it up. Seriously. I'm not making this up, man! I think it was a *Time Magazine* article on research done by Brendan Burchell, sociologist at the University of Cambridge.)

After sharing my positive "Golden Child" tale from a cool and supportive boss, I have a great example of just such a demoralizing attitude from another boss.

Let's take a trip back in time to the chapter where I talked about the graphics database I built. Remember? Chapter three? Ah, has it been so long?

When I constructed that system, I did my best to keep it simple and powerful and efficient. Nevertheless, no cataloging system can be totally intuitive. Photographs. Databases. Labels. Organizational crates. You need some semblance of instructions to train people how to use it. Right?

I came up with a fantastic way to create the instructions - I built a website.

I was very proud of this! Although I have spent many years as a professional Internet developer, websites were a new thing back then, and it was only the second website I had ever constructed.

The site was an awesome way to share the knowledge of using the digital cataloging system. So much better than paper! By building an instructional website, any person in the company could access the data. No hunting for a manual. No searching for paperwork. Just go to the website and there it is.

I was able to include images of the process, photos of the storage bins, screenshots of the database software, and so forth. I explained the workflow of photographing graphics, the proper sequencing to label them, examples of entering the keywords into the database and more. Anyone in the company could easily add data to the archives (or retrieve a graphic from the archive) simply by following the directions on the website.

I tested the effectiveness on an intern who had never touched the system. I picked a graphic for him to find and gave no assistance other than to say, "Read the website and figure it out." Knowing nothing about the system, he found the graphic within about 5 minutes. Perfect!

Very proud of having built such a detailed set of instructions for using the catalog, I excitedly bragged about it to my boss. I couldn't wait to show him! I knew he'd be impressed and proud of my work. Now anyone could use the system! I had created something truly universal and versatile with no barrier to entry for any employee. It was brilliant. It worked flawlessly. I was so stoked and pleased with myself. This was the kind of work that would surely get me a raise! Maybe even a promotion!

Thrilled at having attained and exceeded the expectations of my boss, Mr. Freakingmoron, I smiled and awaited his reaction.

"I hired you to work on graphics, not build websites." He said disdainfully. "If you're not going to do the work I hired you for, I can easily find someone else willing to do it, especially for what I'm paying you."

...What!?

I was devastated.

Was this idiot serious?

How did he expect others to use the graphics system he hired me to build, if I didn't document how to use it and create instructions for it?! This was part of what he wanted me to create! I built this thing on his request! I conceived the entire system based on what he asked me to construct! Didn't he want me to explain how it works?

Could anyone truly be as stupid as him? Could anyone truly be that juvenile? That immature? That uneducated?

I built this amazing library and he threatens to fire me!? After I created something more powerful than he ever expected? After I built an archive more effective than any cataloging system the company had in 50 years of business?

That was the night I went home and immediately started looking for a new job.

How dare he threaten to fire me!

Ugh. The story burns me up even now! How rude!

Threatening people is never a way to make them work harder. It's a way to make them despise you and leave (and call you names in a book many years later). I was out of there. Ungrateful idiot.

After I gave my 2 weeks notice, Mr. Freakingmoron literally never spoke another word to me. Seriously. Two solid weeks he never said a thing to me. Didn't assign me any work. Never said hello. Never said goodbye. Nothing. He completely ignored me. I could pass him in the hall and say, "Good morning!" and he would walk right by as though I didn't exist. Unbelievable. I guess he was astoundingly immature after all.

Incidentally, I was making about $9.00 an hour at that job, I might add.

"I can easily find someone else to do it, especially for what I'm paying you?" So he said. He acted like he was paying me six figures! Freaking moron indeed.

In all honesty though, I don't resent him nearly as much as I pretend to. I actually felt sorry for him. The real reason he was upset is because the world was changing too rapidly for him. He was more than twice my age and he knew nothing about computers. This young punk (me) comes along and starts doing things that he didn't remotely understand. Part of the reason he had such a rude and caustic reaction was embarrassment and intimidation. I could see it in his eyes. I could hear it in his voice. I didn't understand it at the time, but in hindsight, it is clear as day. He was angry because he knew my knowledge about this inevitable technology far exceeded his own and he didn't know what to do about it.

He really wasn't such a bad guy. Every single Mr. Freakingmoron, Mr. Assfog, Mr. Jerkhole, and all the rest, are a part of this magical and mysterious journey of living. I'm grateful for all these characters to grace the stage of my life and play their role.

Even if they were sucky supervillains.

My final tale about praising good work comes from a customer who took the time to praise me in front of my bosses. Remember in the first chapter when I told you about Mr. Phonysmile never appreciating my abilities, but the assistant manager thinking I was Superman?

Well, we had a customer who came to us for some digital photo retouching. Apparently, the customer was very difficult to please and she angrily returned the work 2 or 3 times over the course of a couple weeks, always dissatisfied with the results. It had gotten to the point where the Vice President of the company became involved, trying to ease the tension and satisfy the customer.

We had some talented retouchers there. Apparently none of them were good enough for her expectations.

So, I took a crack at it. Started from scratch and finished the work in a single afternoon.

When the customer got the image the next day, I was called out of the lab to the front counter. That never happened. We lab personnel never interacted face-to-face with any customers. I braced myself, figuring she hated what I did and would start screaming at me too.

Nope.

Apparently, the woman was so pleased with my work, she wanted to meet me and thank me in person. In front of the entire front counter staff, the Vice President, and Mr. Phonysmile, she told them I was an asset to the company. That I accomplished in a day what others failed to attain in weeks.

I couldn't do much other than blush and smile and say, "You're welcome."

I thanked her and let her know it made my day.

Praising good work goes very far. I can not thank that woman enough for making me look so good in front of all those coworkers - even if that darn Mr. Phonysmile still didn't appreciate me afterward.

By extension, I thank you, my lovely readers, for spending these few moments with me and sharing in my tales. This chapter is about giving sincere praise and I can think of no better way to end this book than to share my genuine gratitude with you for reading it.

As I said before, time is our greatest gift. I am grateful for your time and I hope you found it worthwhile to spend these brief moments of this time in your life with me. There are countless books in the world about improving the morale of your workplace. I hope you found this one to be enlightening, enjoyable and inspiring.

With all sincerity, thank you.

(Yes, now that you read the whole thing, I know what you're thinking and you're right. Might be best to give a copy to your boss anonymously. Just slip it under the door of his office after hours.)

NOT SUCKING SUGGESTION #8:

Praise will boost morale far better than idle threats of firing someone. Making threats will only foster resentment, not retention. Let people know they are awesome. Let people know they are amazing. Supportive words of kindness will breed loyalty and dedication. Berating people with threats only instills animosity and job hunting.

THE BOTTOM LINE

(How does this advice translate into profits?)

Praise people for good work with sincerity. Don't give phony compliments. Let them know they are appreciated. Thereby improving retention of quality people, which translates into increased profits.

EPILOGUE

When asked the "secret of their success", successful people often give too much credit to their ambition and too little credit to unforeseen happenstance (in others words... "dumb luck"). Those who excel frequently presume they are smarter than everyone else. They naively believe they created their success from sheer will and wits. Truth is, most of them simply had the stubborn fortitude to endure, until they accidentally stumbled into the right place at the opportune moment. Ambition and intellect had little to do with it. Tenacity is indeed the strongest asset to achieve ones dreams, but there are plenty of driven people in this world who spend a lifetime beating their ambitious little heads into a brick wall, because serendipity refuses to give a sucker an even break. You never hear about those people. You may be one of them yourself.

Therein lies the rift betwixt the bosses and the employees of the world.

The bosses are no better than you. No smarter than you. In fact, many of them are unfathomably stupid and yet they act so darn smug. While you resent their ignorance, they are the ones who never have to worry about money, while you live from paycheck-to-paycheck, scared to death of being out of work.

It's not right. It's not fair. But that's the way it is.

Those things in life which are unjust, we need to change ourselves. Perhaps my own ambitions are too lofty, but I hope this book helps to change a few little things in your life in that way. At the risk of sounding like some darn hippie, I hope this book helps to make people a little less sucky, a little more kind, more considerate. I hope it makes people care a little more about the folks they work with everyday.

As I mentioned in the beginning, this book often presented a facetious and snide attitude, but the underlying concepts are quite sincere and heartfelt and positive. The simple principals outlined within these pages are things I have learned and experienced firsthand over the years. When it comes to being a good and upstanding leader, one who is admired and respected, I've seen it done the right way... and I've seen it done the wrong way.

Despite my tangents of ranting and sarcasm, I hope you folks appreciated these principals and start to apply them to your own business relationships. Those who have personally witnessed the difference in work performance from enthusiastic employees versus the drudgery exhibited among workers enduring a "sucky bossdom" can attest to how worthwhile it is to improve that doldrum atmosphere.

That improvement all starts at the top. As a boss or a manager, you want your team to excel. The better they look and the better they perform, the better you look to your own boss. Therefore, if you take away only one idea from this book, I hope it is this - learn that being a humble servant to your personnel will garner you exponentially better support than being a heartless dictator. Don't believe me? Look at political history since... oh, the start of humanity?

"Kill them with kindness" is the old saying.

It works. But I'd rather say, "Influence the behavior of people by being humbly considerate and respectful."

Same idea.

You know I'm right. Because no matter if you are President of the United States, president of a Fortune 100 company, or the nightshift manager at a convenience store, there was a time when you were lower on the totem pole and endured superiors who simply didn't know the right way to treat people, and they definitely didn't know the best way to treat you. They didn't appreciate you. They didn't recognize your talents. They didn't value your worth.

Don't become like them. Be better than that.

Remember, leaders do not exist to tell you what to do. Leaders exist to assure you have the resources and the power to get things done. They are not in charge. You are. Your fate is in your command. Don't let them suck.

THE 8 "NOT SUCKING" GUIDELINES

1. HIRE PEOPLE SMARTER THAN YOU AND LET THEM DO THEIR JOB

Never feel threatened when subordinates possess more knowledge then you. They are supposed to be smarter than you. That is how your team will excel. Trust them to know what they are doing. They know their job far better than you will ever understand it. Never attempt to dictate workflows and processes. Offer your suggestions. We appreciate that. We want you to take an interest in our work and appreciate our efforts. We want you to help us do our jobs better. That is why you are there. Offer guidance and help.

2. TAKE THIS CHART AND SHOVE IT

Do some real work. Stop planning endless meetings everyday. People who do nothing but plan meetings and never do real work can never be trusted. Your employees are very cognizant of the fact that your position may be a useless squandering of company funds and you need to invent a lot of superfluous meetings and charts and doubletalk in order to make your job appear justified. But if you actually try to be genuinely useful, you will earn far more respect and boundless job security. No smoke up the tush allowed!

3. POWER TO THE PEOPLE

Empower your employees to make decisions and get things done. Give them the chance to take responsibility for their actions and feel they are in control of their destiny. Don't force them to endure the politics of "approvals" from a dozen people. When someone has a genuine need or a great idea, make it happen. Period.

4. GET YOUR HANDS DIRTY

Get in there and help. Assist. Work alongside the people you are in charge of. Get to know them. Whether you are flipping burgers or designing computer graphics or building a skyscraper or driving a bus, get your butt in the field and turn a proverbial wrench (or literal wrench, as the case may be) with your men... Unless you run a gentleman's club and your name is Vinny. Don't get on the pole with the girls. There are exceptions to these rules, dude.

5. PEOPLE BEHAVE THE WAY THEY ARE TREATED

People will behave the way they are treated. Stare over their shoulders and treat them like lazy slackers and guess what - out of sheer resentment, they will gladly meet your expectations. Allow people the freedom to slack off and take things easy and guess what - they will make sure they get their work done out of sheer worry that excessive slacking will prevent them from accomplishing their job expectations. Okay. I'm joking. Hopefully they will get their work done out of sheer appreciation for you trusting their work ethic.

6. PEOPLE WORK WITH YOU - NEVER FOR YOU

Whatever their "job description" might be, people have a heck of a lot more skills and talents and experiences than you realize. Let them utilize those abilities. Don't treat them like robots or machines which are only capable of the singular tasks of their position. You will be shocked at what your teams are capable of attaining when you follow this philosophy. This rule will be the most difficult one for you to obey. Treating people like a cog in the machine is ingrained so deeply into our culture, it will be difficult to see your fellow humans as dynamic and versatile beings. Try. You will find yourself pleasantly surprised.

7. THE WATCHED POT NEVER BOILS

Completing projects on time is important and deadlines should not be ignored. However, when your business allows, don't attempt to dictate *when* the work should be performed. Let people work when they want, as long as they want. Naturally, this doesn't apply to all industries. If you run a bank or a retail store, you are obligated to your customers to be open during the promised hours. But for many fields of work, it's a lot more important to get the job done on time and not *during* a certain time. Does not apply for jobs like paramedics or firefighters - you guys *have* to be on time!

8. PRAISE GOOD WORK

This takes so little effort on your part and it goes a long way. Equally important to being a boss who shows appreciation is being a peer who shows it. I love when bosses say that others appreciate me and speak highly of my work, but it sometimes means even more when a peer says it. Voice your appreciation. Let people know when they do something impressive. Write it down. Document it. Offer proof in writing, so when reviews of work performance come around, your peers can say, "This is what my coworkers think of me..."

 ABOUT THE AUTHOR

Eric Muss-Barnes was going to write his biography in third person until he figured that was just too lame.

I was born and raised 2500 miles outside of Hollywood, in the Rock & Roll Capital of the World. Served a full 12 years hard time in Catholic School and wouldn't trade the good education for anything but immortality.

First job I ever had was in the 6th grade, as a paper boy for *The Cleveland Press* newspaper. *The Cleveland Press* was in business for over 100 years - from November 2, 1878 until June 17, 1982. I started in around September of 1981. Do the math. That's right. After they enjoyed more than a century of business, I lost my first job in 9 months. There went all my video arcade money.

My teenage rite-of-passage jobs were ushering a movie theatre and asking "Would you like fries with that?" for a fast food restaurant. Since then, I've been a professional video director/editor/producer and made an award-nominated short film. I have designed advertisements for multimillion-dollar sales campaigns and invented toys for greeting card companies. My photography has sold in art galleries across the country and I have crewed on an Academy Award Nominated film (look for me in the credits of *American Splendor*). In addition to having multiple short stories published in anthologies, I penned a vampire novel entitled *The Gothic Rainbow* in 1997. Literally. Pen and paper. I wrote it by hand first. 190,000 words, baby. After all that, I moved to California in 2003 with no job and no apartment to seek my fortune and discover where the serendipity of life might lead.

Ended up doing lots of skateboarding. Building websites for movie studios. Photographing bikini models. Dating bikini models. Riding motorcycles. And writing this book. That sort of thing.

I currently live and work in the unicorn sunshine of Los Angeles... and it totally doesn't suck.

COLOPHON

HP Pavilion dm3t Notebook PC

Windows 7 Professional 64-Bit OS

EmEditor Professional 4.13

Open Office 3.2.0

Macromedia FreeHand 10

Adobe Photoshop CS2

Fonts:

    Palatino, BadaBoom BB, Laffayette Comic Pro,

    Action Men, Action Women, Sound FX

www.ingramcontent.com/pod-product-compliance
Lightning Source LLC
Chambersburg PA
CBHW051546170526
45165CB00002B/900